1 MONTH OF
FREE
READING

at

www.ForgottenBooks.com

By purchasing this book you are eligible for one month membership to ForgottenBooks.com, giving you unlimited access to our entire collection of over 1,000,000 titles via our web site and mobile apps.

To claim your free month visit:

www.forgottenbooks.com/free895923

ISBN 978-0-265-83123-6
PIBN 10895923

This book is a reproduction of an important historical work. Forgotten Books uses
state-of-the-art technology to digitally reconstruct the work, preserving the original format
whilst repairing imperfections present in the aged copy. In rare cases, an imperfection in
the original, such as a blemish or missing page, may be replicated in our edition. We do,
however, repair the vast majority of imperfections successfully; any imperfections that
remain are intentionally left to preserve the state of such historical works.

B

MORAVIAN MUSIC FOUNDATION

PUBLICATIONS

No. 3

THE COLLEGIUM MUSICUM SALEM: ITS MUSIC, MUSICIANS AND IMPORTANCE

By
DONALD M. McCORKLE
Executive Director, Moravian Music Foundation

Reprinted from
THE NORTH CAROLINA
HISTORICAL REVIEW
October 1956

THE MORAVIAN MUSIC FOUNDATION, INC.
WINSTON-SALEM, N. C., 1956

THE *COLLEGIUM MUSICUM SALEM:* ITS MUSIC, MUSICIANS, AND IMPORTANCE*

By Donald M. McCorkle

Prefatory Note

Even the most casual reader of Oscar Sonneck's monumental *Early Concert-Life in America* (1731-1800)[1] is instantly impressed by the complex sociological pattern of benefit concerts, dilettantes, itinerant virtuosi, and serious musical amateurs, all seeking to transplant some of Europe's rich musical culture into contemporary America.

Only one phase—but a most important phase—of the history of American music is the story of the Moravians, or more properly the church called *Unitas Fratrum*. These pious people, principally Germans, brought with them the most *vital* musical culture ever to take root in the colonies. Their Pennsylvania settlements (Bethlehem, Lititz, and Nazareth) were oases for the eighteenth-century intelligentsia, both domestic and foreign.

In 1753 the Moravians spread to North Carolina to establish another settlement which they called Wachovia (*recte, Wachau*). The central village was to be Salem, with the smaller villages of Bethabara, Bethania, Friedberg, Friedland, and Hope, all situated within Salem's periphery.

The musical life of the Moravians in Wachovia largely revolved around Salem, as did the Pennsylvania settlements around Bethlehem. Like Bethlehem, Salem's music was primarily sacred (about 80 per cent), but of a different character

* In addition to the references cited in the text and footnotes, see the author's "The Moravian Contribution to American Music," *Notes*, September, 1956; and "John Antes, 'American Dilettante,'" *Musical Quarterly*, October, 1956.
The author wishes to acknowledge the influence and help of the senior musician of Winston-Salem, Mr. Bernard J. Pfohl, who became a nonagenarian on September 13, 1956. His dedicated service to music, especially as a member and director of the Salem Band and the Moravian Easter Band for over a half-century, has enriched his city and his church immeasurably. His infallible memory for dates and events of yesterday is a source of constant amazement and importance to any scholar working with the history of the Moravian Church, South. To him the author expresses his heartfelt thanks.
[1] Oscar Sonneck, *Early Concert-Life in America* (Leipsig [Germany], Breitkopf and Härtel, 1907).

Reprinted from The North Carolina Historical Review, Volume XXXIII, No. 4, October, 1956

from choral music in any other place in eighteenth-century America. Whereas, New England was nurturing the simple Psalm tune and the ingenious fuguing tune, the Moravians were composing elaborate concerted anthems which they accompanied with string quartet, or a larger ensemble consisting of strings, horns, clarinets, trumpets, trombones, and flutes. Perhaps most interesting is the fact that modern musicians are inclined to rank some of this music with the finest of the eighteenth-century choral masterworks.

Having brought some of the earliest instruments to arrive in America, it was only natural that the Moravians would also encourage the practice of secular music, although, of course, to a lesser degree than the music for the church. As Germans, they naturally chose the *Collegium musicum,* that venerable old German amateur society, for their medium for secular music performance, as well as occasional large sacred choral renditions.

But, for whatever type of music, the most distinctive phenomenon of the musical activities of the eighteenth-century Moravians was their need for music as a life-necessity, and not as a cultural veneer.

Quietly reposing among thousands of pages of manuscript sacred music, diaries, and assorted pressed flora in the Moravian Church Archives at Winston-Salem are the remains of the *Collegium musicum der Gemeine in Salem,*[2] the most extraordinary musical society in North Carolina's early history. This organization was the southern counterpart of that in Bethlehem, an ensemble whose performances in Colonial America were highly esteemed by the many statesmen, generals, and foreign dignitaries who heard them. Since the Bethlehem *Collegium musicum* began at a time when its European predecessors were becoming extinct through the dawning era of public concerts, there can be little doubt that the Moravians transplanted the *Collegia musica* to America, and thus prolonged their existence by another century.

The earliest date which can be assigned with certainty to the establishment of the *Collegium musicum Salem* is 1786,[3]

---

[2] "Musical Society of the Congregational Community in Salem," hereinafter shortened to the more frequent title, *Collegium musicum Salem.*
[3] Four works are signed *Collegium musicum der Gem. in Salem,* 1786.

The Salem Archives, built in 1797, formerly the Warden's House.

thereby making it either the third or fourth oldest in the United States.[4]

If it is possible to make deductions from the extant secular music collection—and from some of the original instruments now preserved in the Wachovia Museum[5]—the most obvious conclusion that can result is that this eighteenth-nineteenth century *Collegium musicum* was a very active and versatile aggregation. The music numbers to almost 500 compositions, of which nearly 150 are in manuscript, and runs the gamut from violin duos to "grand" symphonies,[6] and from anthems to oratories. Since the chamber music (including chamber-size symphonies) outnumbers the orchestral by over 300 pieces, it is evident that either the Salem taste inclined to the more intimate forms, or that the size of the ensemble was not equal to performing many works of symphonic proportions. In the course of this article, it will be apparent that both explanations are justified. At any rate, the *Collegium musicum Salem*, whether fully-developed or embryonic, had at its disposal one of the largest and most diversified libraries of secular music of any ensemble in that period of American musical history.

The tastes of these musical amateurs (all of whom were artisans or ministers by profession) reflected the contemporary tastes of Europe, and to some extent of Philadelphia, Charleston, Boston, and New York. The preferred composers were evidently Abel, Haydn, Mozart, and Pleyel. The greater part of the music (which, by the way, was acquired almost as soon as it was published) was early-classic, i.e., from c.1760 to c.1780. Of fully developed Classicism are a few first editions of Haydn and Mozart—from Haydn the Opus 77 String Quartets and symphonies Nos. 80, 89, 93, 94, 99, and 103. Mozart is represented by a quartet (flute, violin, viola, and 'cello) arrangement of *Don Giovanni* (Simrock, 1804), the Second Piano Quartet (K.493), and the symphonies Nos. K.162, 183, 199, and 504.

---

[4] Bethlehem, 1744; Lititz, 1765; Nazareth, c. 1780.
[5] Donald M. McCorkle, "Musical Instruments of the Moravians in North Carolina," *The American-German Review*, XXI, 3, 12-17.
[6] Classical symphonies for large orchestra.

Of the many early Romanticists known to the Salem Moravians, few made any more than a passing entry on the European musical stage. Only the names of Beethoven, Cherubini, Dussek, Lefèvre, Méhul, Weber, Winter, and Wranitzky would be familiar to many present-day musicians. Curiously, the Moravians overlooked Schubert and Mendelssohn, thereby verifying the aesthetic fact that some "masters" can only be recognized and appreciated in retrospect.

JOHANN FRIEDRICH PETER AND THE FIRST AMERICAN CHAMBER MUSIC

While the actual organization of the *Collegium musicum Salem* did not take place (or at least take name) until 1786, there can be no doubt that its modest beginnings occurred as early as 1780, the year in which Johann Friedrich Peter (1746-1813) was sent to Salem as, among other things, music director. And modest beginnings they must have been indeed, for the official church records make little mention of any instrumental music, other than for organ and brass choir, which was performed in the Wachovia settlements. All of this music was, of course, confined to the church services and to chorale playing out-of-doors.

In view of the accuracy of the diaries it is fairly certain that the men recorded as being instrumentalists (again excepting the trombonists and organists) were actually the only ones in Salem.[7]

Evidently to offset the rather heavy emphasis on harpsichord and trombone, other instruments were soon ordered from Europe: 1783-1784, three violins (in accounts spelled

---

[7] Therefore the ensemble in this early period must have been comprised of the following men: Rev. Johann Friedrich Peter—violin, viola (?), clavier, and director; Jacob Loesch, Jr. (moved to Bethania, 1789)—flute; Rudolph Christ—violin and trombone; Carl Ludwig Meinung—harpsichord (he owned one); Johannes Reuz—harpsichord and trombone; Samuel Stotz —harpsichord; and perhaps Johann Krause—viola and trombone. Another violinist was probably the Stokes County Clerk (later governor of Mississippi), Robert Williams, who had to make a fifteen-mile trip into Salem for rehearsals. Proof of his participation would seem to be in two of his editions (dated and signed 1789) which found their way into the *Collegium musicum* collection. Two other probable members were the Rev. Johann Christian Fritz, from Bethabara, clavier; and Lorenz Seiz, who is known only as an organist, but who made five manuscript copies of string trios by Johann Daniel Grimm, a European Moravian.

"füholyne," "fiholine," and "fieholine"); and 1785, two clarini. Since the latter shipment included horns also, it is not impossible that the first viola and violoncello (both preserved in the Wachovia Museum) came at the same time. It is, at least, fairly certain that by 1788 the *Collegium musicum Salem*—and therefore the church also—could boast of at least three violins, a viola, a violoncello, flute, two horns, and two clarin trumpets.

If the amateur performers of this little ensemble given in the Brother's House (or perhaps in the Congregation House) were unpretentious, they did at least have the benefit of working with a fine musician and his music. Johann Friedrich (often called John Frederik) Peter was without doubt the most brilliant of all Moravian musicians, and was never equalled by any other in the succeeding generations. His music collection included copies he had made of symphonies, quartets, etc., by various contemporary European masters. Forty of these manuscripts are extant in the Salem Archives, all left by him for the *Collegium musicum* (and in fact, each bears the signature of both Peter and the *Collegium musicum*), and it is a fact that many of his other copies were taken back to Bethlehem by him in 1790.[8] Since Eitner[9] did not know of the existence of many of the originals represented in this collection, it is certain that some of these copies by Peter are the only existing copies in the world. The composers are: Carl Friedrich Abel, Johann Christoph Friedrich Bach, Johann Ernst Bach, Franz Beck, Karl Heinrich Graun, Johann Daniel Grimm, Nathanael G. Gruner, Adalbert Gyrowetz, Leopold Hoffmann, Franz Josef Haydn, Anton Kammell, Electress Maria Antonia of Saxony, Johann Meder, Franz Xaver Richter, Josef Riepel, Mathias Stabinger, Johann Stamitz, and Joseph Touchemolin. Several other works are anonymous.

In many cases these manuscripts are marked with later editorial corrections and drippings of candle wax, thus verifying their performance in Salem, or at least in America. All

---

[8] Works copied in Salem, then taken to Bethlehem, include a trio for strings by Stamitz, and a Sinfonia for strings by Graun.
[9] Robert Eitner, *Biographisch-Bibliographisches Quellen-Lexicon* . . . (Leipsig [Germany], Breitkopf & Härtel, 1900).

of this music was copied by Peter at an amazing rate of speed, all between 1765 and 1769, while he was attending the theological seminary at Barby, Saxony. For example, six trios by Leopold Hoffmann are signed (signifying dates of completion of copying) successively April 3, 5, 6, 7, 9, 10, 1767.

While many other works (e. g. Haydn, Lidl, Pleyel, Schwindl, Wanhal) were added to the repertoire of the *Collegium musicum Salem* in the late eighties, there can be no doubt that the most important compositions in the history of early American music were written in Salem in 1789.

Johann Friedrich Peter completed his *Six Quintetti à Due Violini, Due Viole è Violoncello* seventeen months prior to his recall to the Northern Province of the Moravian Church. These sparkling quintets, abounding with pre-Classical charm, are unchallenged as the earliest extant chamber works written in America. That Peter wrote these works to order for the *Collegium musicum Salem* is evident by certain technical aspects of the music itself. For, as Hans T. David[10] has observed, the violin and first viola parts are highly virtuosic, while the second viola and violoncello quite calculatedly avoid all technical difficulties. Peter obviously drew his melodic, harmonic, and formal styles from the many, now-forgotten, composers of whose works he made copies. If these works were actually intended for Salem, Peter must have been one of the violists, since no record of more than one viola in Salem until early into the nineteenth century has been found. This may indeed explain the fact that Peter took the score and parts back to Bethlehem, leaving no copy for the *Collegium musicum Salem*.

AN INTERREGNUM

Succeeding Johann Friedrich Peter as musical director were no less than three men: Gottlieb Shober (1756-1838), Johannes Reuz (1752-1810), and Carl Ludwig Meinung (1743-1817). Since each was primarily an organist, there can be no definite indication as to who actually assumed the

---

[10] Hans T. David, "Musical Life in the Pennsylvania Settlements of the *Unitas Fratrum*," *Transactions of the Moravian Historical Society* (Nazareth, Pa., 1942), 40.

directorship of the *Collegium musicum*. A good deal of circumstantial evidence, however, suggests that after Peter the Salem musical directorship became more of a committee project. Of the three, Shober and Meinung, in view of their personal collections of secular music, were probably better fitted for the work, while Reuz, a trombonist and organist, was perhaps more active with the church music.

Beginning with this period, the importing of printed and lithographed music begins in earnest. From 1790 to 1808, no fewer than twenty-eight chamber and fifteen orchestral works (chiefly Andre, Breitkopf & Hartel, and Hummel editions) were added to the repertoire.[11] While the majority are still early-Classic, the trend toward Romanticism is evident by the following composers: Abel, André, Boccherini, Cherubini, Danzi, Devienne, Dulon, Durand, Dietter, Fischer, Fodor, Giordani, Gleissner, Gyrowetz, Haydn, Hoffmeister, Mozart, Pichl, Pleyel, Reinards, Romberg, Schwindl, Vogel, Winter, Wölfl, and Wranitzky. In addition, three of Boccherini's early quartets were brought by Gotthold Reichel in 1802.[12]

A number of chamber works by Boccherini, Devienne, J. Fodor, Klöffler, Vogel, and Wendling, were brought to Salem by Dr. Samuel Benjamin Vierling, who arrived as resident physician in 1790. From all indications, Vierling must have been a capable violinist[13] as well as a gifted surgeon. Most of his music bears a label indicating that it was purchased from "Christian Jacob Hutter's *Musical Repository*, Lancaster, [Pennsylvania]." And, indeed, Hüter accompanied Brother Vierling on his trip to Salem.

In 1805, the *Collegium musicum Salem* was enlarged by two trumpets, two clarinets, and a bassoon—the first woodwinds, other than flutes, to be used in Salem. Of particular interest are the trumpets, for they were evidently *Zinken* made by the Moravian instrument maker, Gütter, of Neukirchen in 1805.[14] Just exactly why the Moravians in Salem

[11] This is, of course, based upon a modern index of the extant collection in the Salem Archives.

[12] Manuscript copies made by J. G. Cunow, Bethlehem, 1776.

[13] His violin is now owned by a descendant living in Greenville, South Carolina.

[14] These instruments, a *Krummer* (curved) and a *Gerader* (straight), are now in the Wachovia Museum.

should have ordered instruments theoretically extinct by a century is not clear. Nor is the fact that Gütter was making them! Four violins were also added to the instrumental music in 1805. The purchase price is interesting: two cost £3.15, and the other two £2.12.6. The second set was perhaps somewhat inferior.

THE ERA OF THE Collegium musicum

Several music receipts would appear to indicate that Gottlieb Shober was still the Salem musical director as late as 1806, although other factors would presumably have prevented this possibility. He was succeeded as church organist by Friedrich Christian Meinung and Gotthold Benjamin Reichel in 1803, and became a state senator in 1805. Never again did he have an active part in Salem life. A receipt dated 1808 attested to the fact that Friedrich Christian Meinung had bought two clarinets ($9.00) in Bethlehem for the Collegium musicum Salem. In this unobstrusive announcement can be found the beginning of the era of the organization, an era which was to see its peak of development and ultimate decline and disappearance. The same receipt is important for another reason: it is the first time that Friedrich Christian Meinung's name is mentioned in connection with secular music, the music which he more than any other person was to bring to its full flowering. A son of a music director of the previous generation, and father of one in the next, Meinung (1782-1851) was certainly the most important musician in Salem during the first half of the nineteenth century. Although he did not assume directorship until 1822 (and then for only eleven months), his influence as a violinist, violist, clarinetist, trombonist, organist, pianist, and vocalist is still apparent today. By profession a school teacher, surveyor, and bookkeeper, he was by avocation a musican of discriminating tastes. While there is, of course, no way of knowing his musical attainments, it is possible to make a prediction based upon his large collection (the greater part of the Collegium musicum collection) of secular music.

Secular music in this period became further removed from the church. This fact can be verified by the observation that five of the finest—and last—Moravian composers,[15] all clergymen, were active in Salem during the first three decades of the century, but none of them seems to have had any direct association with the *Collegium musicum*.

Bishop Johannes Herbst, the most prolific of all American Moravian composers, came to Salem as pastor in 1811 (died in 1812), and brought with him his scores from his fantastically large handwritten collection of anthems, oratorios, cantatas, motets, and masses. Since most of the individual parts, excepting those for a number of oratorios, were left in Lititz, Pennsylvania, there is scant possibility of this music having been performed in Salem, at which time the members of the *Collegium musicum* would have participated. Four probable exceptions would be Handel's *Messiah*, Graun's *Te Deum Laudamus*, J. A. P. Schulz' *Maria und Johannes* (some sections of which became part of the *Gemeine* Collection), and Wolf's *Ostercantate*.

Bishop Jacob Van Vleck, who succeeded Herbst as pastor in 1812, was a polished violinist; but he, likewise, did not perform with the ensemble. He did, however, bring two editions for the enrichment of Salem's secular music. The most important of these bears the awkward title:

Tre Trii,/ per due / Violini and Violoncello,/ Obligato./ Dedicati a Sua Excellenza il / Sigre G.J. de Heidenstam,/ Ambassatore de Sa Maj il Ri de Suede a Constantinopel./ Composti a Grand Cario dal/Sigre Giovanni A-T-S./Dillettante Americano. /Op. 3. [-London, J. Bland . . . 45 Holborn, n.d.]

The rather cryptic name, "Sigre. Giovanni A-T-S," belonged to the American-born Moravian missionary, John Antes (1740-1811), who served in Cairo from 1770-1781. Antes returned to England in 1783, and probably soon after sought out Bland, the publisher. As Bland very obligingly moved in 1795, it is certain that the trios were published prior to that year.

[15] Johann Christian Bechler (1784-1857), Johannes Herbst (1735-1812), Simon Peter (1743-1819), Jacob Van Vleck (1751-1813), and Peter Wolle (1792-1871).

Curiously, no complete set of these works has thus far been located anywhere in the world. Only two partial sets are known in the United States; the Salem copy lacks one page of the violoncello part, while the Sibley Musical Library's lacks the entire first violin. Three sets of initials on the Salem copy indicates that it was brought by Jacob Van Vleck, and later passed on to Shober, then to Alexander Meinung.

An old legend in the Moravian settlements says that Antes was acquainted with and played trios or quartets with Haydn. There is little doubt that such a meeting did occur, although no verification can be found. Antes' nephew, the English bishop, Christian I. Latrobe, was inspired by Haydn's suggestion to compose a set of piano sonatas, which he did and dedicated to the master. And he also wrote an account of his friendship, which was published posthumously in 1851.[16]

Antes himself supplied some circumstantial evidence when, in his paper to the *Allgemeine musikalische Zeitung*,[17] he referred to Haydn's impressario, Johann Salomon, as *"mein Freund, Hr.* Salomon in London.*"* Antes must have been a very capable violinist,[18] judging from the keen violinistic insight he used in writing these trios—as well as his numerous accompanied anthems and songs.

The musical emphasis of the *Collegium musicum Salem* now turned to orchestral works in the early nineteenth century, a change made possible by the increased number of string and woodwind players growing up in—or moving into—Salem. Between 1808 and 1825, approximately fifty-two editions were added; of these, thirty-five were for orchestra. Haydn was still favorite; but the tendency seems to have been to follow the newly developing trends (which, by the way, helped to cause the ultimate decline of the whole unique Moravian tradition). Few of the following composers are ever heard of today: Ahl, Beethoven, Braun, Dressler, Dussek, Gerke, Goepfert, Gyrowetz, Haydn, Hen-

---

[16] E. Holmes, "The Rev. C. I. Latrobe," *Musical Times* (London), Sept. 1851.

[17] Leipsig, July 16, 1806, No. 42.

[18] A violin, inscribed "Johann Antes in Bethlehem, 1759," is in the Moravian Historical Society Museum, Nazareth, Penna.

kel, Kotzwara, Kummer, Hupfeld, Lefèvre, Lessel, Mèhul, Paër, Pleyel, Polledro, Romberg, Rösler, Sterkel, Stumpf, Tulou, Viotti, Winter, Wölfl, and Wunderlich.

Numerous musical receipts record the arrival of not a few clarinets, string instruments, and of course, many reeds, strings, rosin, bows, etc. in the 1820's. Certainly, also significant is the fact that two local artisans, William Holland and Karsten Petersen,[19] were repairing violins, violas, and cellos in the period. In 1820, the musicians requested the Church Elders to consider the purchase of a drum; this request was denied, however, because the drum would be offensive! The first double bass was brought in 1829.[20]

Among the last music to be imported were some woodwind pieces called *Parthien,* or *Pièces d' harmonie,* a form very much en vogue in Europe. The most interesting of these, from the standpoint of American music, are seven works by the American Moravian, David Moritz Michael (1751-1827), who was primarily responsible for the golden era of the Bethlehem *Collegium musicum.* While in Bethlehem, Michael wrote fourteen *Parthien* and two suites for a basic combination of two clarinets, two horns, and bassoon.

Of these sixteen works, apparently only seven were copied and sent to Salem: the suites, and *Parthien* Nos. 1, 2, 4, 5, and 9.[21] While some of these pieces are quite pedestrian, a few can be singled out as works of art. Michael achieved, within his modest means and the limitations of contemporary instruments, works which fairly well show the transition style between Classicism and Romanticism. The works are harmonically and melodically traditional, but use very few ornaments, and abound in melodramatic surprises, and are above all typically German.

For example, the first movement of the *Parthia* No. 1 deserves special attention because of its main theme. This theme, taken from some unknown source, was also used by

---

[19] The author has found a home-made violin which was undoubtedly made by Petersen and it is displayed in the John Vogler House in Old Salem.

[20] Made by H. G. Gütter (or at least sold bv him), Bethlehem, Penna. ($50.00).

[21] *Parthia* No. 9 is not extant elsewhere.

Meyerbeer some thirty years later in the "March" to his opera, *Le Prophète!* Since Michael returned to Europe in 1814, and presumably taking the *Parthia* score with him, it is not impossible that he and the famous opera composer may have met.

Much difficulty is encountered when attempting to establish the membership of the *Collegium musicum* in this period. Meinung was succeeded as music director in 1823 by Dr. Friedrich Heinrich Schumann (1777-1862) and Wilhelm Ludwig Benzien (1797-1832). Since Benzien was a violinist, and only sixteen years old, we may assume that the leadership was actually entrusted to the doctor—as the following document may show.

The only document thus far discovered that specifically concerns the *Collegium musicum* is a sharply worded protest to the Church Elders Conference, dated February 23, 1823:

The hindrances which, by some persons unknown to us, have been placed in the way of the Music Society established by our Brethren and Sisters regarding the playing of customary concerts on Sundays in the Boy's School House, brings us to the following positive clarification, which we want to notify to all those who are interested. We cannot help seeing the unquestionable right of the *Collegium musicum,* or the majority of the same, to appoint themselves the place and the manner of their musical meetings as long (as) nothing happens which is against the rules of Synod or community regulations.—By these rules alone, but not by the false imputation and ill-intentioned remarks, we want to be judged, and not controlled in our performance. If against our presumptions, the Board gives a willing ear to our anonymous slanderer and lays on us an intollerable control, we would find it necessary, even if unwillingly, to withdraw and we will not have any part of playing church music for a congregation which willingly listens to ill-remarks by a slanderer. An irresponsible compliance with these wicked claims will only increase this vice and make it worse.[22]

This was signed by H. Schumann, Chas. F. Levering, J. H. Leinbach, W. L. Benzien, W. Craig, and Georg Foltz. This letter is valuable for several reasons. First of all, it smacks of

---

[22] Manuscript in the Salem Archives (author's translation).

/Portrait by an unknown artist of Wilhelm Ludwig Benzien (1797-1832), one of the Directors of the *Collegium Musicum Salem*.

Dr. Schumann's typical vituperative relationship with the church, and, therefore, could perhaps be dismissed as a "crank letter." Secondly, we are informed for the first time that "customary concerts" were given on Sundays in the Boy's School (built 1794), and that ladies were somehow connected with the organization. Thirdly, it can be inferred that the Church administration looked somewhat askance at secular music performances, which, indeed, would explain the paucity of documentary material relating to them. Finally, and perhaps most significantly, this letter reveals the mounting tensions between the Church and the Community, and thereby the impending decline not only of the *Collegium musicum*, but also of the whole Moravian social system. Such a protest could not have been uttered a decade earlier without fear of expulsion from the *Gemeine* — the church-community. From the very brief, but uninformative, acknowledgment of this letter in the Church diaries, it is obvious that the answer, given orally, was conciliatory. None of the musicians withdrew as they had threatened. Dr. Schumann, himself, was to continue his personal bickering and bargaining for more personal liberties — which he usually got — for many years.

The first and last public performances of the *Collegium musicum Salem* to gain any notoriety (though undoubtedly somewhat due to the spasmodic newspaper service) were two performances of Haydn's *The Creation* in 1829 and 1835. The first performance must have been quite an event, if we are able to give any credence to the editorial-letter which appeared in the Salem *Weekly Gleener:*

With peculiar pleasure we understand that an association of the musicians of this place and vicinity, to the number of between 30 and 40, has been formed, and preparations are making for the performance of that divine Oratorio, *The Creation*, by Hayden [sic].

The cultivation and encouragement of the fine or liberal arts in a society, while they tend to awaken the dormant faculties of youthful talent and genius, and instead of lounging in idleness or roaming for mischief, incite to industry and laudable emulation, teach the mind its proper superiority over the common senses of life, by rendering it sensible of higher aims and nobler enjoyments, those intellectual pleasures, of which, as rational

beings, we have been made susceptible by an all-wise and benev-
olent Creator.

The fine arts, whilst they, like the best of things, may be
prostituted to the worst of purposes, if properly applied, tend
to exalt the mind, and raise the soul in grateful aspirations
toward its fountain-head, its Creator and its God.

We do not recollect ever having heard of an attempt in this
State, perhaps not of any in the southern regions, of performing
this master-piece of musical composition, by so full and respectable a body. The high abilities of some individuals, and the
exertions of all those concerned, justify our expectations of a
good and masterly performance; and we hope that a numerous
and respectable audience will be ready to applaud and reward
so commendable an undertaking.

A Votary.[23]

A subsequent announcement in the same newspaper speci-
fied that the performance would be held in the village
church [24] on the Fourth of July by the "full corps of Instrumental and Vocal Musicians of Salem." Fifty cents was to
be charged for admission. Directing the performance was
either Meinung or Benzien. Since Benzien was officially the
director of the Collegium musicum in this year, and since
Meinung probably sang the role of "Raphael" as he did six
years later, we may assume that Benzien was in charge of
this performance. We have no way of knowing if any profit
was realized, but it is recorded [25] that the total expenses
amounted to $40.00 — ten dollars to Meinung for making
the vocal parts, and thirty to Blum [26] for printing the text.

The orchestral parts used in this first southern performance [27] were copies of copies that Johann Friedrich Peter
had made for the first American performance in Bethlehem
in 1811.[28] It is doubtful that Salem could have used all of
the twenty-three parts (two violins, two violas, two 'cellos,
two flutes, two oboes, two bassoons, contra bassoon, two
clarinets, two horns, two clarini, three trombones, and tim-

---

[23] Weekly Gleener (Salem), April 14, 1829.
[24] Now Home Church on Salem Square.
[25] In music receipts in the Salem Archives.
[26] John C. Blum, publisher of the Weekly Gleener.
[27] No record of an earlier performance in the South has been published.
[28] Attention is here called to M. D. Herter Norton's excellent article,
"Haydn in America (before 1820)," Musical Quarterly, April, 1932.

pani) in Peter's score for this occasion.[29] The English translation used in the Peter manuscript may well have been taken
from that apparently made by Johannes Herbst, which is
to be found in his edition (keyboard reduction) by A. E.
Müller.[30]

The 1835 performance was advertised in *The Farmer's
Reporter and Rural Repository*[31] as being given "by the Members of the 'Society of Amateurs' at Salem." It was again
given in the Church (October 17), but this time the admission was "gratus." F. C. Meinung, *"Director,"* announced
that "the *text* will be sung according to the *original,* but for
the accommodation of those who do not understand the
German language, *English* texts have been prepared, which
may be had at 5 cts. a piece [*sic*]." The profits amounted to
$11.25.

Fortunately, one of the German textbooks preserved lists
the soloists beside their respective roles.[32] They were
"Raphael," F. C. Meinung; "Uriel," Dr. Schumann and Henry
Schultz; "Chorus," Louisa Belo (!); "Gabriel," Antoinette
Bagge and Anna Keehler Crist; "Adam," F. C. Meinung;
"Eva," Lisette Meinung. Members of the chorus were not
recorded, but it is more than likely that the majority of them
are included in a list of all (?) church singers in Salem,
1830-1850, prepared by Edward W. Lineback, c.1850.[33] Although Meinung was credited with the directorship by the
newspaper advertisement, the present writer has been in-

---

[29] These parts became the property of F. C. Meinung; now preserved in
Salem Archives.
[30] Published by Breitkopf & Härtel; now in Salem Archives.
[31] *The Farmers Reporter and Rural Repository* (Salem), Oct. 5, 1835;
successor to the defunct *Weekly Gleener.*
[32] In the autograph of F. C. Meinung.
[33] *Sopranos:* Sophia Behan, Sophia Pfohl, A. Leinbach, Elizabeth Boner
Crist, Sophia Blum Brietz, Tracy Belo Siddall, Louisa Belo Bahnson,
Antoinette Bagge Brietz, Frances Benzien, Susan Rights Keehlin, Hermena
Benzien, A. Keehler Crist, Mrs. Crist, Emma Susseman Stewart, Mrs.
Meinung, Elizabeth Schuman, Mrs. Peterson, Sarah Ann Lineback, Sophia
Zevely, Louisa A. Van Vleck, Lisetta Van Vleck, August Hall Winkler,
Matilda Winkler Siewers, Joseph Siddall Hauter, Sarah Hall Tise, Anna
Clauda Lineback, Adalaide Herman, Louisa Herman, Addie Meinung, D. S.
Ebert; *Tenors:* F. F. Crist, Theo. Keehler, C. F. Schaaf, S. Th. Pfohl,
Gottlieb Byhan, A. F. Pfohl, Dr. C. F. (?) Schuman, Hy. Schultz; *Basses:*
Rudolph Christ (d. 1833), J. Crist, Dr. C. D. Keebler, M. E. Grunert, H. T.
Bahnson, E. A. Ebert, Rt. Rev. J. G. Herman.

formed by a grandson of one of the singers[34] that it was actually Dr. Schumann.

The orchestra probably consisted of many of the following available musicians:

Violins: F. C. Meinung, Henry Leinback
Cello: Charles Levering
Violas: F. C. Meinung, J. C. Jacobson
Basses: Charles Brietz, J. C. Jacobson
Flutes: Henry Leinback, Ephriam Brietz
Clarinets: Levin R. Brietz, T. F. Crist, W. Leinbach, F. C.
    Meinung
Bassoons: Joshua Boner, Charles Levering
Horns: Georg Foltz (1st), Theophiles Vierling
Trumpets: ?
Trombones: ?

The amount of instrumental doubling in this ensemble must have created quite a display of acrobatics!

Finally, the post-mortems as reported by *The Farmer's Reporter and Rural Repository* (October 24):

> Haydn's grand Oratorio of *"The Creation"* was performed in our village on Saturday last, according to appointment, by the musical amateurs of this place, much to the edification of a respectable audience—principally ladies!

This may well have been the final performance of the *Collegium musicum der Gemeine in Salem,* if indeed the chapter had not closed a few years previously. Several times in this period the terms *"Music Gesellschaft"* and "Musical Society" are encountered, thus implying that the last of the German *Collegia musica* had finally given way to the dawning era of brass bands and public concerts, just as its European ancestors had done over a century before. Thus ended the most extraordinary musical culture in the South in the eighteenth century.

---

[34] Bernard J. Pfohl, Winston-Salem, January, 1955.

Date Due

A pen sketch by Mrs. Martha H. Farley from a stone lithograph of a drawing by Gustavus Grunewald in 1839. Seen from Academy Street (Winston-Salem), looking east are (left to right) the Boy's School (built in 1794 and now the Wachovia Historical Museum); the Inspector's House (built in 1812 and now the Administration Building of Salem College); and the Home Moravian Church (consecrated November 9, 1800, and in continuous use since).

9 780265 831236